What's it like to live in ...?

Canada

by Catherine Little

HODDER
Wayland

an imprint of Hodder Children's Books

Other titles in the What's it like to live in? series:

France   Italy   Jamaica

© 2003 White-Thomson Publishing Ltd

Produced for Hodder Wayland by
White-Thomson Publishing
2/3 St Andrew's Place, Lewes, East Sussex BN7 1UP

Published in Great Britain in 2003 by Hodder Wayland,
an imprint of Hodder Children's Books.

Editor: Kay Barnham
Designer: Tim Mayer
Consultant: Lorraine Harrison
Language consultant: Norah Granger – Former head teacher
and senior lecturer in Early Years Education at the University
of Brighton.
Picture research: Shelley Noronha – Glass Onion Pictures

British Library Cataloguing in Publication Data
    Little, Catherine
    What's it like to live in Canada?
    1. Canada - Social life and customs - Juvenile literature
    2. Canada - Social conditions - Juvenile literature
    I. Title II.Barnham, Kay
    306'.0971
ISBN 0 7502 4359 7

Printed and bound in China

Hodder Children's Books
A division of Hodder Headline Limited
338 Euston Road, London NW1 3BH

Picture acknowledgements
Canola Council of Canada 15; Corbis (Steve Prezant) 23;
Eye Ubiquitous (Mike Allwood-Coppin) 8, (L Fordyce) 19,
20; HWPL (Chris Fairclough) cover, 11, 12, (Chris
Fairclough) 25, (Canada House) 26; Impact Photos (Alain
Evrard) 21, (H Hughes) 17, (Steve Parry) 27, Popperfoto 13,
(John C Hillery) 22, (Jim Young) 24; Robert Harding Picture
Library 18; Sylvia Cordaiy 9; Travel Ink (Ronald Badkin) 4,
(Mathieu Lamarre) 10; WTPix (Chris Fairclough) 6, 7, 14,
Map artwork: The Map Studio.

Every effort has been made to trace copyright holders.
However, the publishers apologize for any unintentional
omissions and would be pleased in such cases to add an
acknowledgement in any future editions.

*With thanks for D'Arcy's love and encouragement and for
the help of family and friends for the scrapbook items – CL*

Contents

Where is Canada?

Canada is part of North America. It is a large country bordered by the sea and by the **USA**. The capital city is Ottawa.

Canada is famous for its cold winters and beautiful **scenery**.

Only 30 million people live in Canada, but millions more visit the country every year.

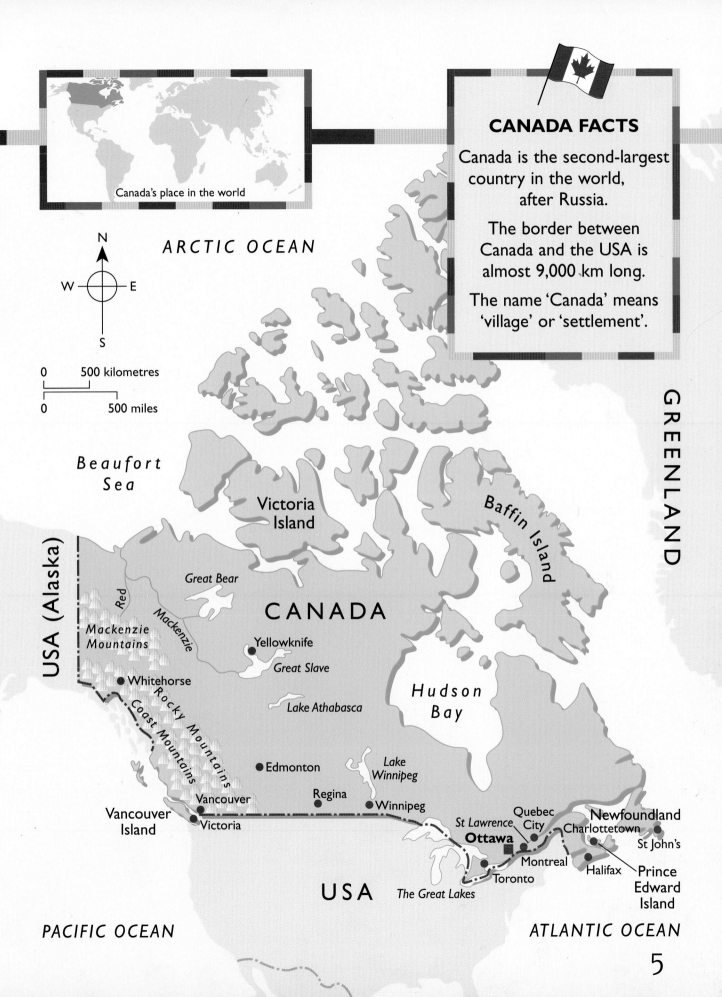

Canada's place in the world

ARCTIC OCEAN

N
W E
S

0   500 kilometres

0   500 miles

GREENLAND

Beaufort Sea

Victoria Island

Baffin Island

Great Bear

CANADA

Red

Mackenzie

USA (Alaska)

Mackenzie Mountains

Yellowknife

Great Slave

Hudson Bay

Whitehorse

Rocky Mountains

Lake Athabasca

Coast Mountains

Edmonton

Lake Winnipeg

Vancouver

Regina

Winnipeg

Quebec City

Newfoundland

Vancouver Island

Victoria

St Lawrence

Ottawa

Charlottetown

St John's

Montreal

Prince Edward Island

Toronto

Halifax

USA

The Great Lakes

PACIFIC OCEAN

ATLANTIC OCEAN

5

Cities

Most cities are in the south of the country, where it is warmer. The largest cities are Toronto, Montreal, Vancouver and Ottawa. Fewer people live in the cold northern cities of Whitehorse and Yellowknife.

Nearly five million people live in Toronto.

Canada has two **official languages** – English and French. Many people speak both languages.

Canada has a **multicultural population**.

The landscape

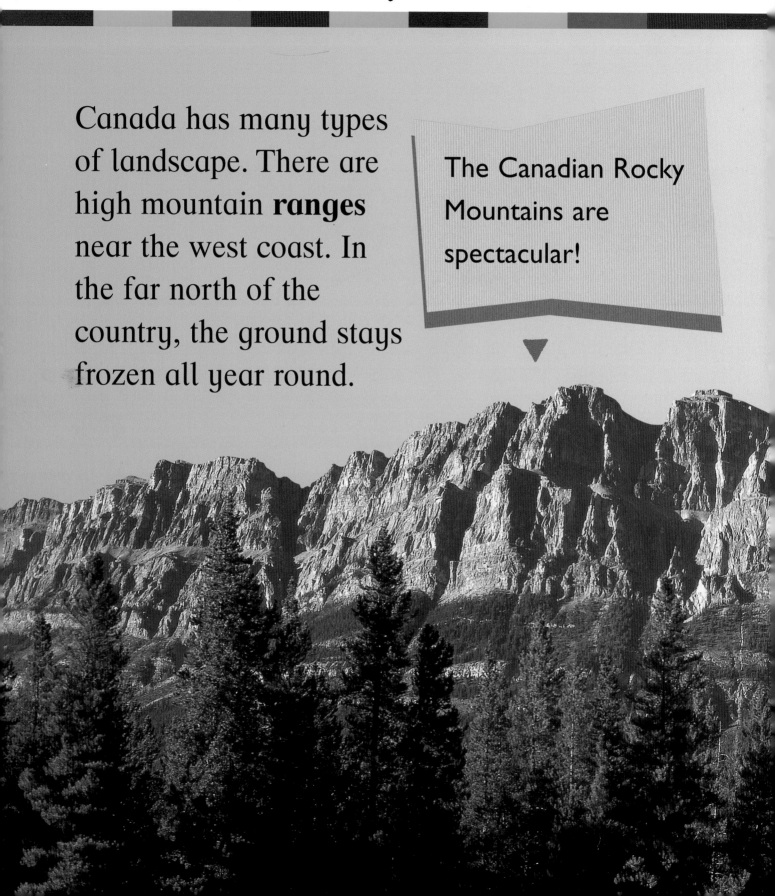

Canada has many types of landscape. There are high mountain **ranges** near the west coast. In the far north of the country, the ground stays frozen all year round.

The Canadian Rocky Mountains are spectacular!

Prairies and forests stretch across central and eastern areas of Canada.

The middle of Canada can be very flat.

The weather

In Vancouver on the west coast, summers can be warm and pleasant.

The west coast of Canada has cool winters, while summers are often hot. Eastern Canada has colder weather, with icy winters and warm summers.

In northern areas, snowdrifts are common.

Further north, **temperatures** can be very low indeed. Winters are bitterly cold, with heavy snow. However, summers are a little warmer.

11

Transport

The Trans-Canada Highway runs right across the country.

People travel around Canada by plane, train, car and bus. The country is so large that it can take five days to drive non-stop from one side to the other.

In big cities, most people travel on buses, trams or underground trains. **Public transport** is so good that people often leave their cars at home.

When it is snowy, snowmobiles are a fun way to travel.

▼

Farming

In Canada, farms can be very large. Farmers need machinery to produce big crops of wheat, fruit and vegetables.

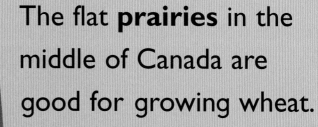

The flat **prairies** in the middle of Canada are good for growing wheat.

Canada is one of the
world's largest producers
of canola – a plant used
to make oil. The word
'canola' comes from the
words 'Canadian' and 'oil'.

Golden-yellow
fields of canola
can be seen along
many highways.

Food

Picnics are popular when the weather is hot and sunny.

People have come from many different places to live in Canada. Restaurants serve food from all around the world, to suit any taste.

Maple **syrup** is made in Canada from the **sap** of maple trees. Many people like to pour it on to pancakes at breakfast time.

It takes a lot of sap to make a small jar of maple syrup.

17

Shopping

People who live in big cities have lots of different places to shop, including large **shopping malls** and small corner stores.

In the West Edmonton Shopping Mall, there are fantastic **exhibits** as well as hundreds of different shops.

▼

Sometimes farmers travel to the nearest city to sell their food.

In small towns, people used to shop by ordering things from catalogues. Now, **Internet shopping** is becoming much more popular.

Houses and homes

Some Canadians **rent** their **apartments**. Other people own their homes. Sometimes renting is cheaper than buying a home. Many Canadians would like to own their own homes, but find it too expensive.

In Newfoundland, homes made of wood are popular.

These modern-looking
apartments are in Montreal.

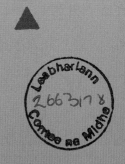

There are different types of homes
in Canada, such as boathouses
on the water. **Architects** design
imaginative new apartments too.

21

At work

Luxury cars are built at this Canadian factory.

Most people in Canada live and work in cities. Others have jobs in factories. Very few people now work on farms in the countryside.

Some Canadians choose to start their own businesses. Many people now work with computers in offices or at home.

Working from home is popular.

23

Having fun

Ice hockey is Canada's national winter sport.

During the winter, Canadians enjoy sports such as skiing, ice skating and **tobogganing**. Many love to play and watch ice hockey.

With so many beautiful lakes to choose from, boating is popular.

When the weather is warmer, **amusement parks** and beaches are busy. Some children spend their holidays at summer activity camps in the country.

Festivals

The Caribana Festival is held in Toronto every year.

Each year, different **festivals** are held all over Canada. These include a comedy festival in Montreal and a children's film festival in Toronto.

Canadians often celebrate their national day with fireworks.

Canadians celebrate Victoria Day in May and Canada Day on 1 July. They might have a picnic or barbecue during the day. There are amazing firework displays at night.

Canadian scrapbook

This is a scrapbook of some everyday Canadian things.

A badge from a shoe museum in Toronto.

This is a postcard of the CN Tower in Toronto.

Canadians use Canadian dollars and cents.

There are a hundred cents in a dollar.

Canadian travel tickets.

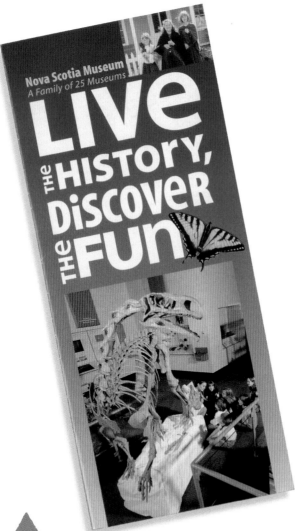

A leaflet for some museums in Eastern Canada.

This entry ticket allows one person to go up the CN Tower.

Glossary

Amusement parks Large outdoor areas with fairground rides and other fun things to do.

Apartments Flats.

Architects People who draw plans for new buildings and then make sure that they are built properly.

Exhibits Special displays or pieces of art for people to look at.

Festivals Times of celebration.

Imaginative When an idea is new and original.

Internet shopping When people use a computer to order things that they want to buy.

Multicultural When people follow customs and habits from many different places and cultures.

Official languages Languages used on a country's official documents.

Population The people that live in a certain place.

Prairies Large areas of flat ground.

Public transport Buses, trains and other types of transport that are available for everyone to use.

Ranges Rows of mountains or hills.

Rent To pay for the use of something.

Sap The sweet juice found inside a plant or tree.

Scenery Natural features of a landscape, such as mountains and lakes.

Shopping malls Large buildings with lots of shops inside.

Syrup Thick, sticky liquid that is used to make food taste sweet.

Temperature A way of measuring how hot or cold it is.

Tobogganing Sliding over snow on a light vehicle with runners.

USA United States of America.

Further information

Some Canadian words

anglophone	someone who mainly speaks English
click	kilometre
elevator	lift
francophone	someone who mainly speaks French
gas	petrol
pants	trousers
pop	fizzy drink
poutine	chips covered in cheese and gravy
runners	trainers
trunk	boot (of a car)
touque	knitted woollen cap
washroom	toilet

Books to read

Only in Canada!: From the Colossal to the Kooky (Wow Canada!) by Vivien Bowers (Firefly Books Ltd, 2002)

Walk with a Wolf by Janni Howker (Walker Books, 1997)

For older readers

Anne of Green Gables by L. M. Montgomery (Puffin Books, 1964)

Index